Mel Bay's

Guide to Guitar
Chord Progressions

by Mike Christiansen

1 2 3 4 5 6 7 8 9 0

Visit us on the Web at http://www.melbay.com — E-mail us at email@melbay.com

Contents

Introduction

The purpose of this book is fivefold:
1. Assist in learning to change chords quickly, accurately, and smoothly.
2. Help guitarists become familiar with chord progressions commonly used in various styles.
3. Train the ears to hear and identify common chord progressions.
4. Provide a foundation for writing original music.
5. Present a variety of accompaniment techniques which can be used to play music in many different styles.

This book is not a dictionary of chord voicings or a 'chord finder.' It is assumed you are already familiar with the fingerings of the chords used in the progressions. If you do not know some of the chords in an exercise, refer to the "Chord Simplification" section near the front of this book.

The chords used in the progressions may be fingered many different ways. The chord voicing used will be left up to you. You may want to try each progression using several different voicings of the same chord. By doing this, you will not only become familiar with the sound of the progression, but you will also be learning new chord fingerings and how to connect those chords accurately and smoothly. Supplementing this book with a book of chord voicings and fingerings might be helpful.

Chords In Various Keys

The progressions in this book are presented by "key." At the beginning of each section is a list of the basic chords found in the key. The chart below shows an example of the the various chords found in the key of D with their Roman numeral assignment.

I	ii	iii	IV	V	vi	VII°
D	Em	F$\sharp$m	G	A	Bm	C$\sharp$dim

Notice the chords are listed in alphabetical order beginning with the name of the key and proceeding through the major scale of that key. A Roman numeral is written next to each chord name indentifying the chord. Major chords are represented with large Roman numerals and minor chords are represented with small Roman numerals. For example, the ii chord in the key of C is Dm. Assigning Roman numerals to the chords in a given key is also very helpful in training the ear to hear chord progressions. Eventually, you will be able to identify the chord in a piece by its Roman numeral. In every major key, the I, IV, and V chords are major chords and are identified using large Roman numerals. The ii, iii, and vi chords are always minor and are written using small Roman numerals. The VII chord in the key is a diminished chord.

The seven basic chords in any major key can be identified by first starting with the letter name of the key and writing (in alphabetical order) the notes of the major scale. The chords in the key will have the same letter names as the notes in the scale. Next, assign the notes of the scale Roman numerals (I-VII). Remember, the I, IV, and V chords will always be major (indicated by large Roman numerals); the ii, iii, and vi chords will be minor (indicated by small Roman numerals); and the VII chord will be a diminished chord.

The following charts show the seven basic chords in the various major and minor keys. Notice, in the minor keys, the i and iv chords are minor; the III, V, and VI chords are major; the ii chords is usually a m7♭5; and the VII chord is diminished.

Chart Of The Chords In Each Key

Major Keys

I	ii	iii	IV	V	vi	VII
A	Bm	C#m	D	E	F#m	G#dim
B♭	Cm	Dm	E♭	F	Gm	Adim
B	C#m	D#m	E	F#	G#m	A#dim
C	Dm	Em	F	G	Am	Bdim
C#	D#m	E#m	F#	G#	A#m	B#dim
D	Em	F#m	G	A	Bm	C#dim
E♭	Fm	Gm	A♭	B♭	Cm	Ddim
E	F#m	G#m	A	B	C#m	D#dim
F	Gm	Am	B♭	C	Dm	Edim
F#	G#m	A#m	B	C#	D#m	E#dim
G	Am	Bm	C	D	Em	F#dim
A♭	B♭m	Cm	D♭	E♭	Fm	Gdim

Minor Keys

I	ii	III	iv	V	VI	VII
Am	Bm7♭5	C	Dm	E	F	G#dim
B♭m	Cm7♭5	D♭	E♭m	F	G♭	Adim
Bm	C#m7♭5	D	Em	F#	G	A#dim
Cm	Dm7♭5	E♭	Fm	G	A♭	Bdim
C#m	D#m7♭5	E	F#m	G#	A	B#dim
Dm	Em7♭5	F	Gm	A	B♭	C#dim
E♭m	Fm7♭5	G♭	A♭m	B♭	C♭	Ddim
Em	F#m7♭5	G	Am	B	C	D#dim
Fm	Gm7♭5	A♭	B♭m	C	D♭	Edim
F#m	G#m7♭5	A	Bm	C#	D	E#dim
Gm	Am7♭5	B♭	Cm	D	E♭	F#dim
A♭	B♭m7♭5	C	D♭m	E♭	F♭	Gdim

Transposing

By substituting chords in the various progressions with chords from another key having the same Roman numeral assignment, the progressions in this book can be transposed and played in any key. For example, the first progression in this book uses C and G7 chords. C is the I chord in the key of C and G7 is the V chord in the key of C. The same progression may be transposed and played in another key by substituting the I chord and the V chord from another key. For example, A (the I chord in the key of A) and E7 (the V chord in the key of A) could be substituted for the C and G7 chords. If you transpose a progression, you will notice that it has the same relative sound in each key.

Chord Embellishments

Chords other than major, minor, augmented, and diminished (such as 7, m7, add9, etc.) are embellishments of basic chords. Chord embellishment refers to 'spicing up' the basic major and/or minor chords by adding more notes to make the chords richer and give them more color. For example, G7 has a more colorful sound than does a plain G chord. The information in this section of the book will show what can be added to the basic chords in a key to make the chords sound richer. When playing by ear, a knowledge of chord embellishment will help in finding the exact chord to use rather than a chord which is merely close.

The first step in chord embellishment is to identify the seven basic chords in the key. As was shown earlier in this book, this can be done by writing the major scale and assigning the correct Roman numeral to the steps of the scale to find the basic major, minor, and diminished chords in the key. For example, the chart below shows the seven basic chords in the key of D.

D	Em	F#m	G	A	Bm	C#dim
I	ii	iii	IV	V	vi	VII°

After assigning the basic chords in a key a Roman numeral, use the chart below to find what embellishments can be added to the chords in the key. For example, in the key of C the IV chord is F. So, in the key of C you can use Fmaj7, F6, Fadd9, or any of the other embellishments for the IV chord.

I, IV	Major, 6, maj7, add9, maj9, sus, 6/9, maj7$\sharp$11
V	Major, 7, 7^{sus}, 9, 11, 13, $7^{\flat 5}$, $7^{\sharp 5}$, $7^{\flat 9}$, $7^{\sharp 9}$
ii	minor, m7, m7sus, m9, m6, $m7^{\flat 5}$, m+7
iii, vi	minor, m7, m7sus, m9, m+7
VII	dim

One of the most frequently used embellishments is to play the V chord as a 7th chord. For example, in the key of G, it would be very common to use a D7 chord rather than a D chord.

Knowing how to embellish chords is also invaluable in writing your own chord progressions. Practice writing chord progressions in several keys using the basic chords, and then go back and embellish the progression.

Chord Simplification

The chord progressions in this book, and in any other music for that matter, can be simplified by reducing the chords. Chords may be simplified by omitting embellishments. The rules of chord embellishment may be used in reverse. Chords which have a number lager than seven can be reduced to 7th chords. For example, a C13 chord could be reduced to a C7 chord.

In Seventh chords which have a sharp and/or flat number in them (such as D7b5), the sharp and/or flat number may be omitted. Such as, G7b5#9 being reduced to G7. Seventh chords may also be reduced to simple major chords.

Minor seventh chords may be reduced to minor chords. Minor type chords with a number larger than seven in their name can be reduced to m7 chords. For example, Dm9 or Dm7sus could be reduced to Dm7, or even Dm. Suspended chords (sus) and 7sus chords can be simplified to major and 7 chords.

Embellished chords from the major chord family (6, maj7, maj9, 6/9, add9) can all be reduced to major chords. As a rule, 13th chords can be reduced to 11th chords, 11th chords can be reduced to 9th chords, 9th chords to 7th chords, and 7th chords reduced to major chords.

Chords with added bass notes or chords over bass notes are written with a chord name followed by a slash and a note name. For example, D/C# indicates to play a D major chord with a C note in the bass. These chords can be simplified by simply playing the chord name on the left. For G/F#, you could play G.

If many chords appear in one measure, the music can be simplified by omitting some of the chords. In 4/4 time, if more than two chords appear in a measure, keep the chords to be played on beats one and three. The other chords are passing chords and can be omitted if necessary. In the example below, the circled chord would be kept.

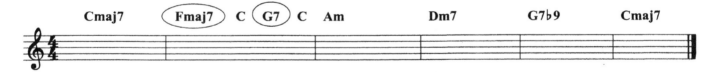

If more than four chords appear in one measure (chord changes on the half beats), play only the chords which fall on the first half of the beat. The chord changes can be simplified even further by playing only the chords on beats one and three. In the following example, the music could be simplified by playing the circled chords when there are two chords to a beat.

In 3/4 time, if more than two chords appear in a measure and you want to simplify the music, play only the chords which fall on beats one and two. If necessary, the chord on beat three can be omitted. By playing the circled chords in the following example the chords could be simplified.

Chords Outside Of The Key

Chords other than the seven basic chords within a key may be used in chord progressions. *Secondary dominants* are chords which are not in the key but may be used in a chord progression. For the purposes of this book, a secondary dominant is a chord, which is normally a minor chord in the key, has been changed to a seventh chord. Secondary dominants are usually followed by the chord from within the key which is five letter names lower than the name of the secondary dominant. For example, in the key of C there is suppose to be an Am chord. It can be changed to an A7 chord, and the chord following the A7 will most likely be Dm.

In some styles of music (particularly rock and contemporary styles), it is common to use the chord which is one whole step lower than the name of the key. For example, in the key of D it would be common to use a C chord even though it is not found in the key of D.

In still other styles of music, particularly jazz and Latin styles, it is common to have a key change appear in the progression. This is done without a change of key signature. These key changes are fairly easy to spot. When a series of chords (usually a m7, or m7b5, followed by a 7th, then a major, maj7, or m7) appear which are unrelated to the original key, a key change has occured. An example of this key change appears in the progression below. The key change has been circled.

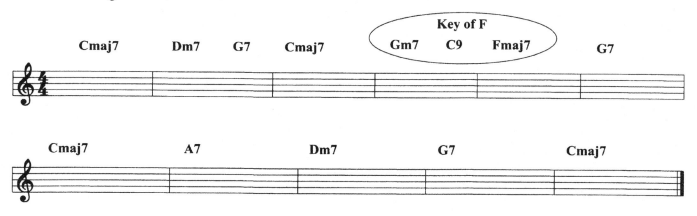

For the purposes of this book, all chords (even if a key change occurs) will be assigned a Roman numeral relating to the original key.

Accompaniment Patterns

Although there is not a set rule for which chords may be used in a particular style of music, certain chord progressions are commonly used in various styles of music more than others. The exercises in this book have been grouped according to style. Written in the first one or two measures of each exercise is a strum or fingerpick pattern which could be used to play the exercise, and be stylistically correct. These patterns take one or two measures to complete and may be repeated and continued throughout the entire exercise. Remember...these are only suggestions. You may use whatever strum, fingerpick, or any other type of accompaniment pattern you wish.

The accompaniment patterns which are written at the beginning of each exercise in this book, can be used to play other music in the same musical style from sheet music and/or song books, as well as the excercises in this book.

The strum patterns are written using strum bars, and the fingerpick patterns are written in tablature. Written below are the various strum signs and their equivalent time values.

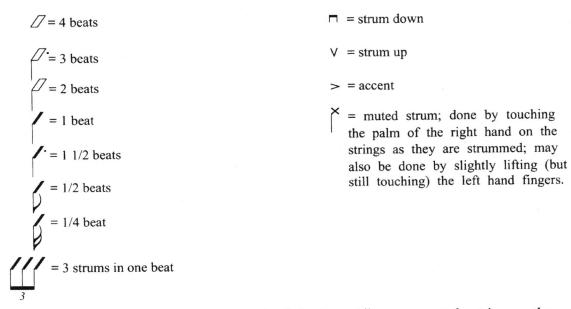

In the tablature for the fingerpick patterns, the six horizontal lines represent the strings on the guitar. The top line is the first string, and the bottom line is the sixth string. The letters on the lines indicate which right-hand finger picks the string.

    p=thumb
    i=index finger
    m=middle finger
    a=ring or third finger

With the fingerpick patterns, when a letter is placed on a line, play that string with the right-hand finger indicated by the letter. The stems on the letters indicate the rhythms. For example, the following pattern could be used to play two beats of a G chord.

The term *comping* refers to a type of accompaniment in which the strums are separated by rests rather than a steady stream of strums. These short one or two measure strum rhythms are sometimes referred to as *comp patterns*. Comping is commonly used in a jazz style. Written below is an example of a comp pattern. This pattern takes one measure to complete and can be repeated in each measure of a piece of music in 4/4.

Some of the exercises in this book have comp patterns written at the beginning of the exercise. Remember...these comp patterns can be used to play the exercises in this book as well as any other music in the same style.

Common Chord Progressions

Knowing which Roman numerals are assigned to the chords in a key will be helpful in learning some common chord progressions. A *progression* is a series of chords. Written below are some of the more common chord progressions. These progressions are popular because the chords sound as though they lead or 'progress' smoothly to the next chord. For example, the V chord often goes to the I chord because that chord change has a resolving sound. The chords in the key won't always be played in the order shown below, but these progressions happen frequently enough that you should be aware of them. Because the progressions are written with Roman numerals, they can be applied to any key. Written in the parentheses next to each Roman numeral is the name of the chord if the progression were in the key of G. Train your ear to hear these progressions. Start simple. For example, learn what a I chord going to a I chord sounds like in every key. This ear training will be very helpful in learning to play by ear. Practice playing these progressions in every key. Strum each chord as many times as you like, or use strumming, fingerpicking or comp patterns.

V(D) ⟶ I(G)

IV(C) ⟶ V(D) ⟶ I(G)

ii(Am) ⟶ V(D) ⟶ I(G)

vi(Em) ⟶ ii(Am) ⟶ V(D) ⟶ I(G)

iii(Bm) ⟶ vi(Em) ⟶ ii(Am) ⟶ V(D) ⟶ I(G)

Practice the following progressions written in various musical styles. After playing the exercises as written, transpose them into other keys. As well as playing the accompaniment patterns written in the first one or two measures, try using other familiar accompaniment patterns. Also practice repeating the exercises using different chord voicings consistently playing the chord changes smoothly and keeping them positioned close to one another.

Key of C

Chords in the Key of C

C	Dm	Em	F	G	Am	Bdim
I	ii	iii	IV	V	vi	VII°

Progressions In C

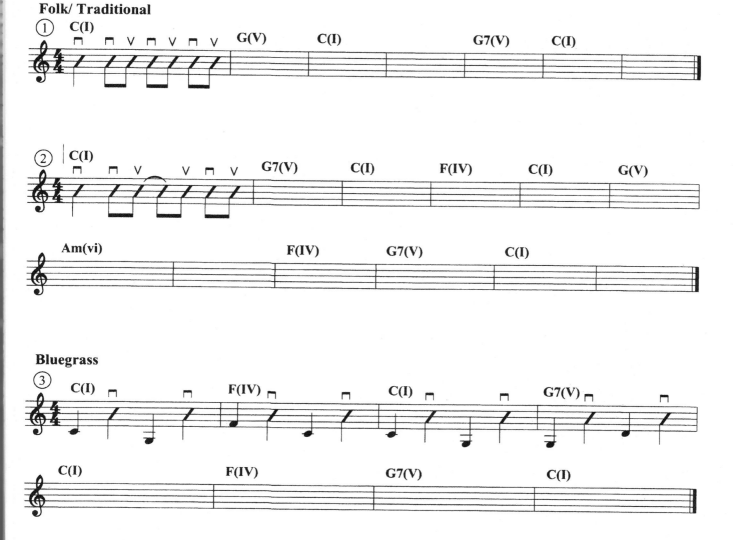

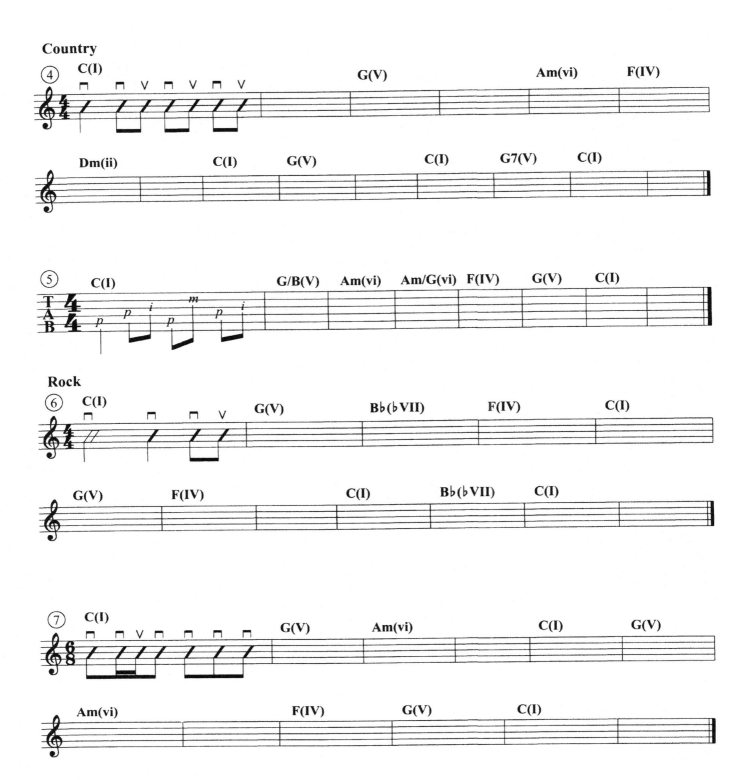

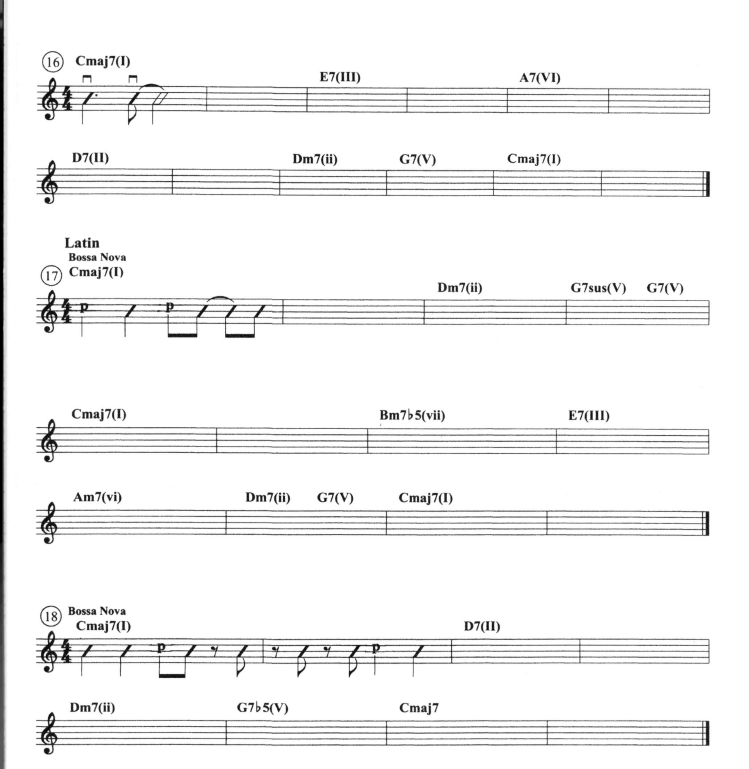

*The letter "P" indicates to pick the lowest string of the chord with the right- hand thumb. For example, for a C chord, pick the fifth string. The strum (/) is done by pulling strings 2, 3 and 4, or strings 1, 2 and 3 with the first, second, and third fingers of the right hand.

Ragtime

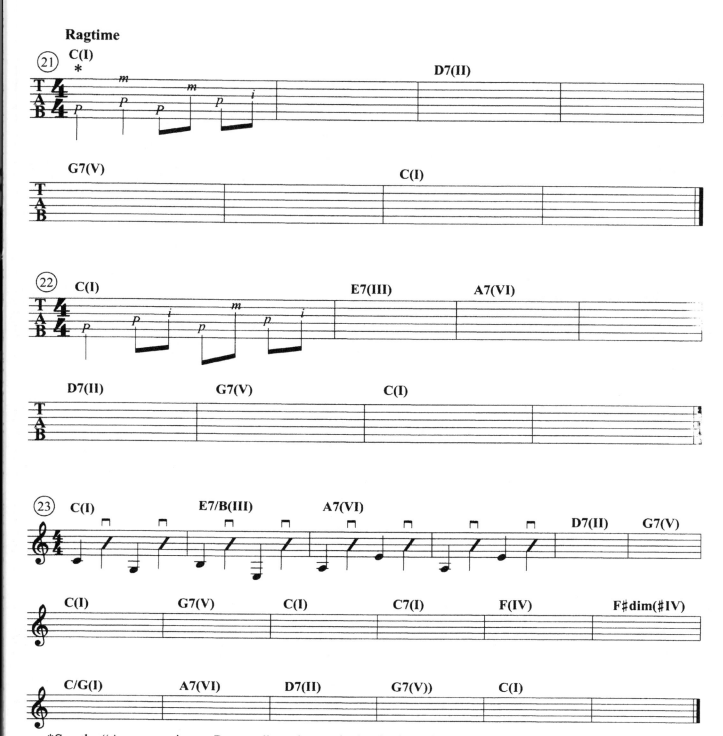

*See the "Accompaniment Patterns" section at the beginning of this book.

Reggae

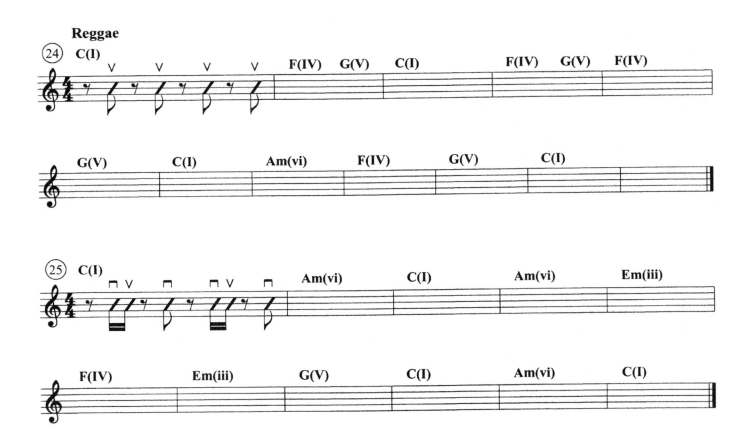

Key of A minor
Chords in the Key of A minor

Am	Bm7b5	C	Dm	E	F	F#dim
i	ii	III	iv	V	VI	VII°

(Most Commonly used chords are i ii iv v)

Progressions in A minor

Key of G
Chords in the Key of G

G	Am	Bm	C	D	Em	F#dim
I	ii	iii	IV	V	vi	VII°

Progressions in G

26

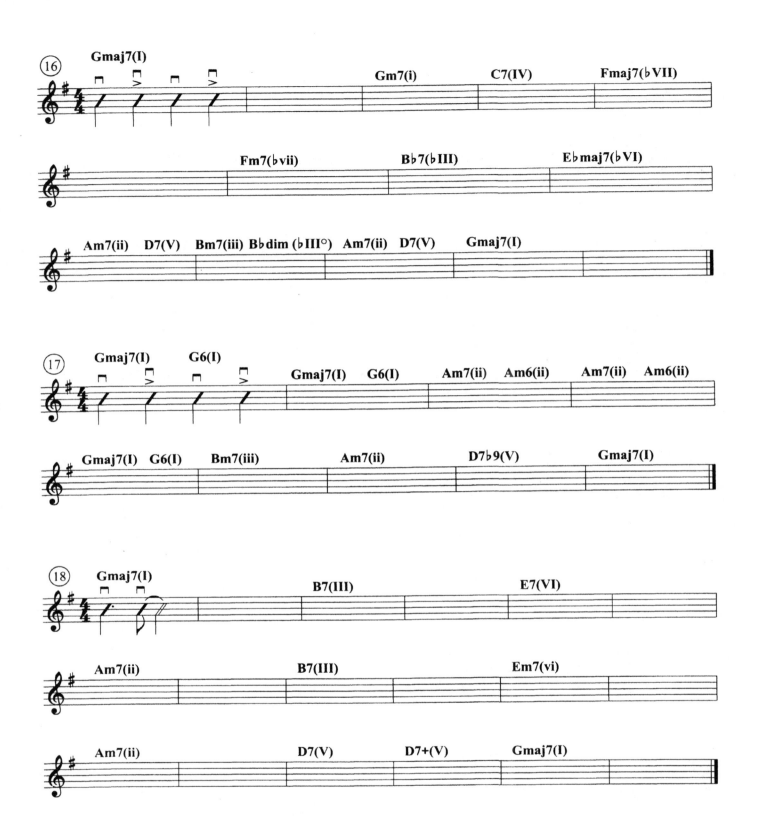

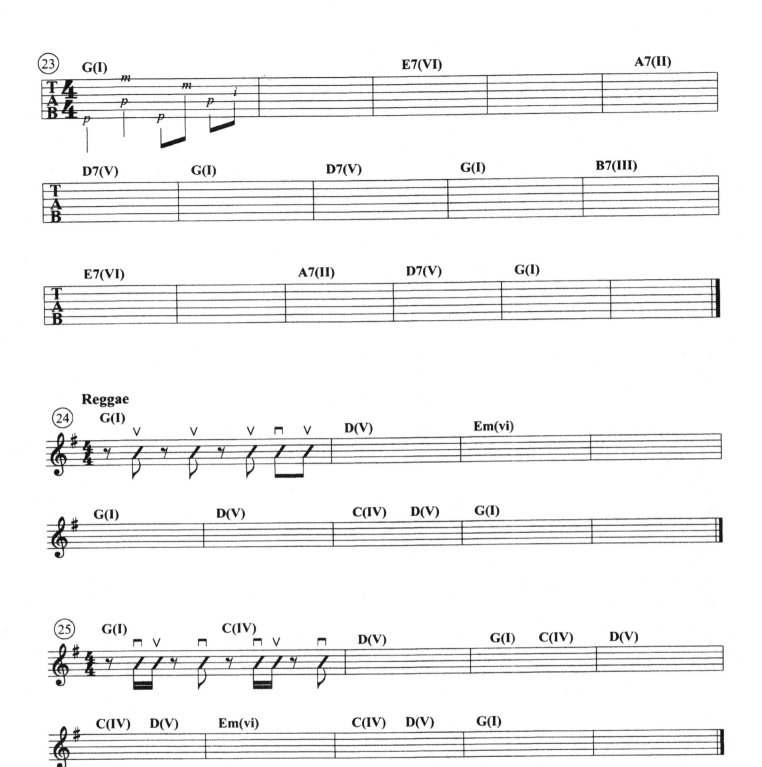

Spanish

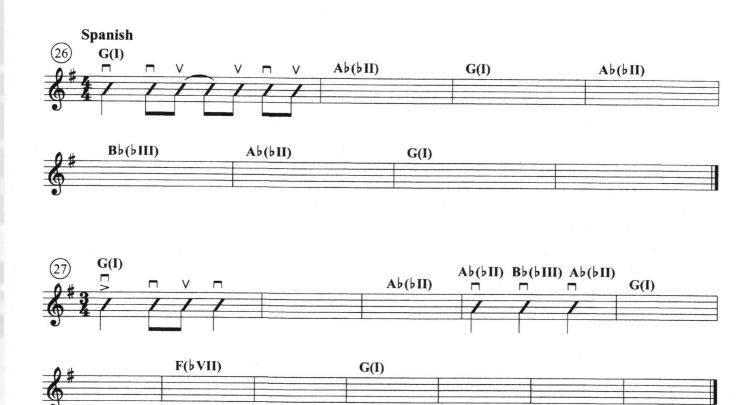

Key of E minor

Chords in the Key of E minor

Em	F#m7b5	G	Am	B	C	D#dim
i	ii	III	iv	V	VI	VII°

Progressions in E minor

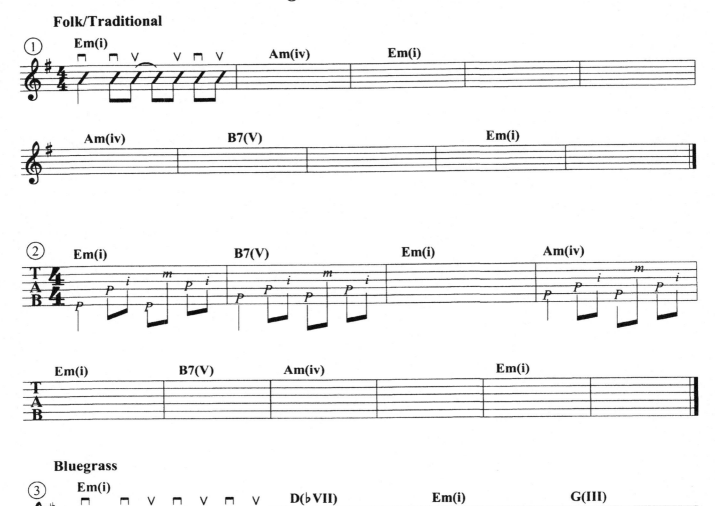

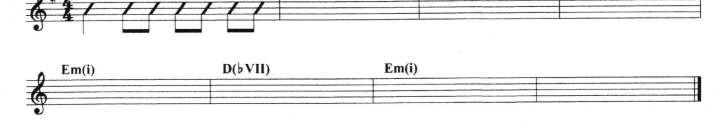

34

Ragtime

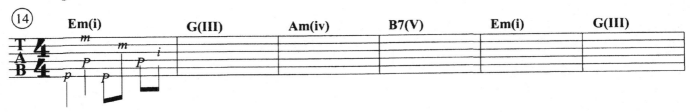

⑭ Em(i)   G(III)   Am(iv)   B7(V)   Em(i)   G(III)

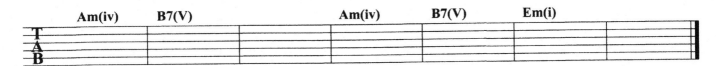

Am(iv)   B7(V)   Am(iv)   B7(V)   Em(i)

Reggae

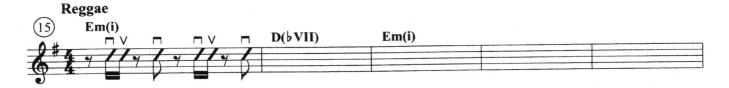

⑮ Em(i)   D(♭VII)   Em(i)

D(♭VII)   Em(i)   G(III)   D(♭VII)

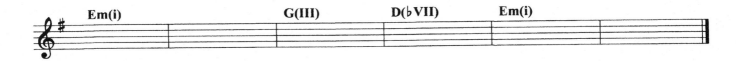

Em(i)   G(III)   D(♭VII)   Em(i)

Spanish

⑯ Em(i)   D(♭VII)   C(VI)   B7(V)   Em(i)   D(♭VII)

C(VI)   B7(V)   Em(i)   B7(V)   Em(i)

Key of D

Chords in the Key of D

D	Em	F#m	G	A	Bm	C#dim
I	ii	iii	IV	V	vi	VII°

Progressions in D

39

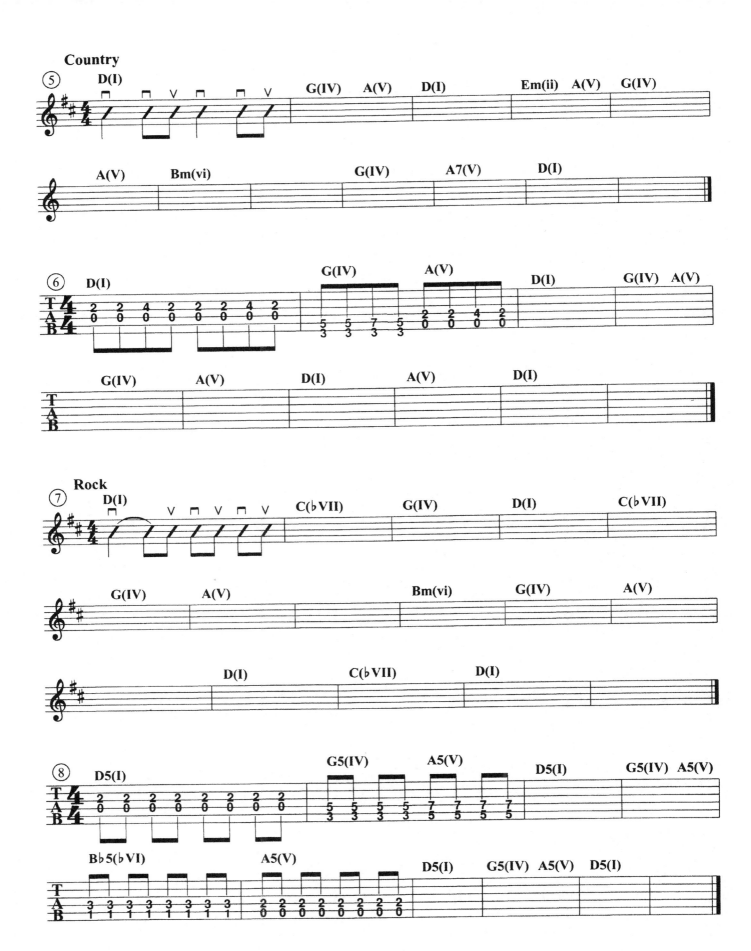

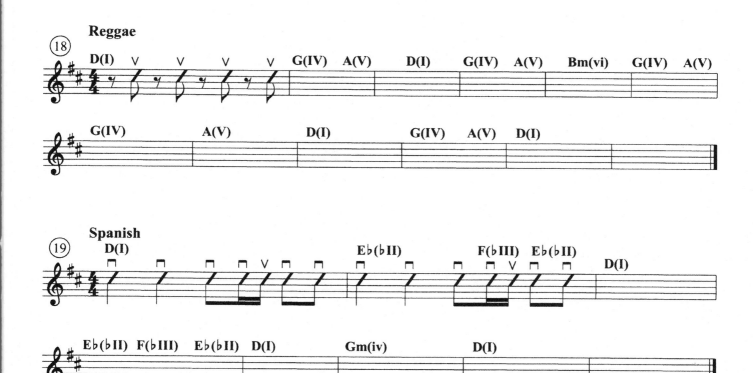

43

Key of A

Chords in the Key of A

A	Bm	C#m	D	E	F#m	G#dim
I	ii	iii	IV	V	vi	VII°

Progressions In A

45

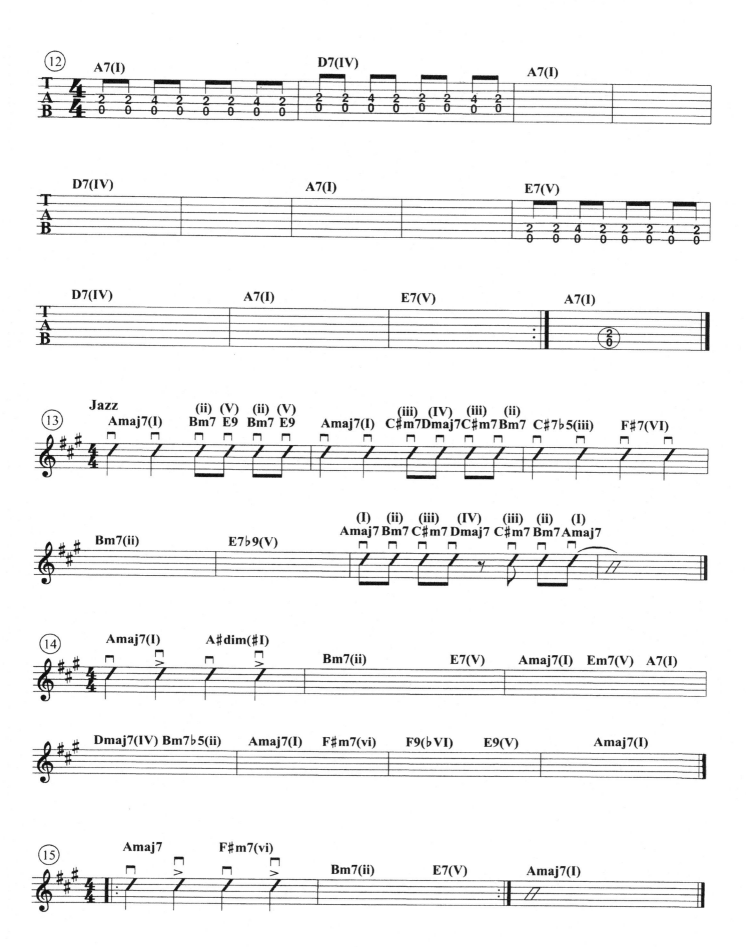

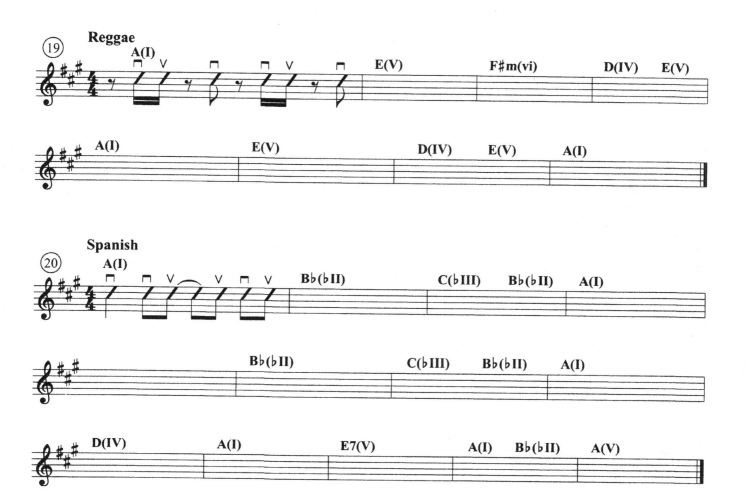

Key of D minor

Chords in D minor

Dm	Em7♭5	F	Gm	A	B♭	C#dim
i	ii	III	iv	V	VI	VII°

Progressions In D minor

50

Jazz

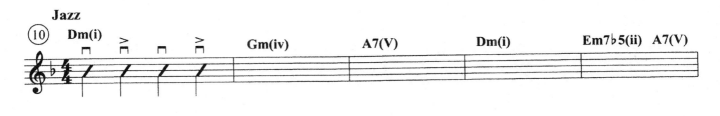

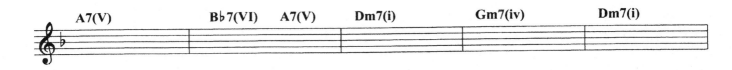

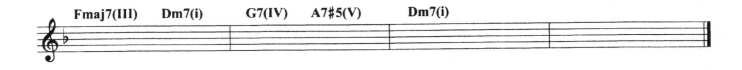

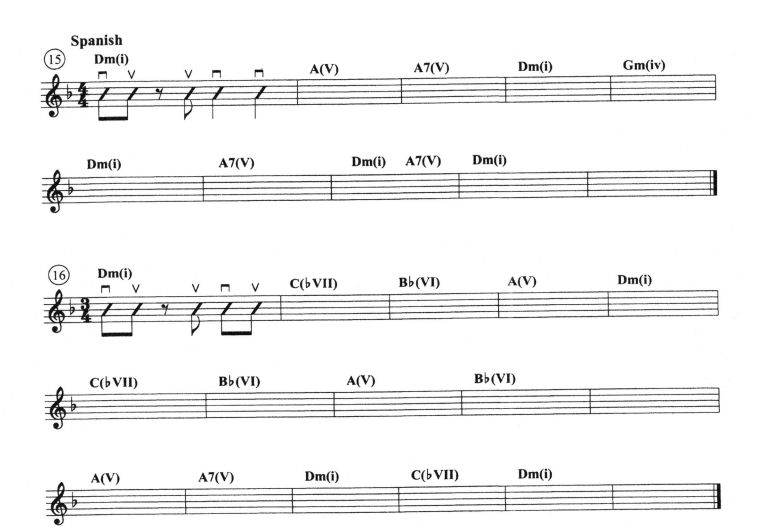

Great Music at Your Fingertips

Printed in Great Britain
by Amazon

24274717R00033